The Torriano Sequences

by

John Heath-Stubbs

pictures by

Emily Johns

Hearing Eye
1997

Published by
Hearing Eye
Box No. 1,
99 Torriano Avenue
London NW5 2RX
1997

ISBN 1 870841 50 6

Typeset by Jayne Clementson
Printed in Great Britain by Aldgate Press, London E1

PREFACE

It was, if I remember rightly, in the summer of 1987 that my old friend John Rety came to see me. He explained that he was planning a series of small poetry pamphlets which he intended to publish (his press eventually became known as Hearing Eye). These pamphlets were to be accompanied by illustrations and decorations by Emily Johns. Had I, he asked me, anything suitable to offer him? It so happened that I had recently written a series of parodies (half a dozen in all) in which the cats associated with the English poets were made to speak, employing (as one might suppose) the styles of their human companions. I had not been quite sure what to do with these, for they might throw out of balance the book of new poems I was planning for my principal publishers, the Carcanet Press. Thus the first of these Hearing Eye pamphlets, *Cats' Parnassus*, was born. It had a certain success, going into three editions in six months – for the English are notoriously crazy about animals – especially cats, dogs and horses. Hearing Eye editions were going ahead, producing collections – often of young and unknown poets who thus had a chance to make their debut in the poetry world.

The next year John Rety asked me if I could do another series. A possible idea might have been *Dogs' Helicon*. The dogs of English poets include Alexander Pope's 'Bounce' (but Norman Ault has shown that Pope owned two dogs successively with this name). Then there was Cowper's companion, the spaniel 'Beau' who picked for him a water lily the poet could not reach (I think 'Beau' belonged to the Throgmorton family, but Cowper took him for walks). I don't know the name of Wordsworth's dog who was trained to go before him while the poet, composing out loud, walked along the Lakeland roads. The dog would turn back and warn him if anybody was coming. Then there was Byron's dog 'Boatswain', Emily Brontë's 'Keeper' and Matthew Arnold's two dachshunds 'Geist' and 'Kaiser'. Elizabeth Barrett Browning's 'Flush' had already been taken care of by Virginia Woolf. There was in addition a very unpleasant, snappy fox-terrier called 'Wessex' belonging to Thomas Hardy, a great poet doubtless, but no favourite of mine. But somehow this idea did not gel for me. Dogs, I felt, if they could talk would speak not in poetry but in prose – as indeed 'Flush' did for Virginia Woolf. I make a present of this scheme to anyone who thinks they could carry it out.

Instead of this I chose a new series of poems on clocks and other *Time Pieces* (1988), and this was followed by *A Partridge in a Pear Tree* (1988) based on the old Christmas song, and also printed as a series of cards. For no particular reason it seemed amusing to let the letter 'C' continue to play a role in the titles – so next we had *A Ninefold of Charms* (1989) then *The Parson's Cat* (1992) (an allusion to a Victorian parlour game) and finally *Chimaeras* (1994). These are here collected in one volume. Most of them were introduced to the public in readings at the Torriano Arts Meeting House in Kentish Town – a venue where many poets have had the opportunity of reading new work in public for the first time. It has been kept going for a number of years, often under difficult circumstances. Therefore the overall title of *The Torriano Sequences* seemed appropriate enough.

These are, for the most part, light poems – though I hope nobody still believes in the old Victorian distinction between 'serious' poetry and 'light verse', the latter occupying a certain below-stairs position in the mansion of Apollo. But I've touched on some graver subjects – the nature of man and animals, of time and eternity and on the monsters which the sleep of reason breeds.

I trust these subjects are not too esoteric. I detest being called erudite, and – a thieving magpie – I make no claim to learning. I hope these poems may amuse, perhaps instruct. Let the reader judge.

John Heath-Stubbs
12th December 1996

CONTENTS

CATS' PARNASSUS

HODGE

Where Arts, where Sciences, their reign extend,
One truth is clear – the cat has been man's friend.
In all the feline race – the humble tabby,
The alley Tom, with coat adust and shabby,
Cats sprung from fruitful Egypt's nobler breed
(Honours divine were once for these decreed),
Cats whiter than the snow, cats black as night,
Cats formed to be a Persian queen's delight,
The tailless Manx, the blue-eyed cats of Siam –
You'll nowhere see a finer cat than I am:
Old Hodge, whom learned Johnson chose, to share
His plain commodious mansion in Gough Square.
By night I, vigilant, patrol the house,
Swift to repress each sly, invading mouse,
Who might with scrabblings mar his wonted rest,
Or in his papers build her procreant nest;
By day, while he is poring on his book,
I sleep contented, in the ingle-nook,
Till Anna Williams shall dispense the tea –
I hope there'll be some oysters too for me.

JEOFFREY

For I will consider my master Christopher

For he also is the servant of the living God

For he yowls at all hours singing psalms

For he is of the house of Asaph the chief musician

For all poets are of the royal household of David

For deprived of ink and paper he scrawls verses on the door
of his prison with a key

For he prays naked in the rain – but I do not accompany him
in this

For I have too much concern for my fur which is the robe
of honour the Lord has given me

For he has no passion for clean linen, and is lousy

For he could seek better instruction from me in these matters

For maybe he spares his lice out of charity

For the Lord created them from the dust of the earth

For the Lord created Adam from the red clay

For man and louse are brothers before the mercy seat

For he is called Smart for he smarts from the whips of
his keepers

For he is called Christopher for he also is a bearer of Christ

Let Smart, house of Smart, rejoice with poor Jeoffrey,
his good cat –

For the cherub cat is a term of the angel tiger.

SELIMA

On this pretentious vase's side,
Which someone in bad taste has dyed
    With bogus Chinese flowers,
I, Selima, recline, and wish
That I could catch those silly fish;
    I've waited here for hours.

I'm Mr Walpole's cat, and hate
To live in pseudo-Gothic state
    High up on Strawberry Hill;
Then there's that Mr Thomas Gray,
Who'll poetise me one fine day –
    I'm jolly sure he will!

I am a normal sort of cat,
Unintellectual at that –
    Who keeps her talons sharp,
And has got nous enough to know
Those goldfish, swimming to and fro
    Are just up-market carp.

But still, to fill my hungry maw
A whisker first and then a claw –
    Worth venturing, I think!
But this fine-glaze chinoiserie
Is much too slippery for me –
    I'm going in the drink!

Come, Tom, come Susan, quick I say!
Come, Mr Walpole, Mr Gray –
    I thought you were my friends!
Save me, or I shall soon be dead –
The waters close above my head –
    Nine times. My story ends.

FOSS

My master is called Edward Lear,

Of ways unsalubrious and queer,

And I, his cat Foss,

Am quite at a loss

To fathom that runcible Lear.

ATOSSA

Great Atossa, sleek and fat –
I am Matthew Arnold's cat,
With my eye on that absurd
Little bright canary-bird.
Poor Mathias is his name –
I regard him as fair game;
But, to my disgust and rage,
He's quite safe inside his cage;
So I sit and watch him – thus
Might have sat Tiberius –
Dreaming how I'd love to crunch
His small, fragile bones for lunch.

Visions of another kind
Rise from my ancestral mind –
Plains and mountains of Iran,
And the towers of Isfahan;
All the tales Ferdousi sings
In his chronicle of kings:
Sohrab dying on the sand,
Stricken by his father's hand,
Where the stars arise and gleam
On the mighty Oxus stream.

But, those arbiters of fate
Trusting, I just have to wait.
Life, my master Matthew claims,
Thwarts our sick, divided aims:
I don't feel that way at all –
Needs no spark from heaven should fall.
One day, careless servants are
Bound to leave that cage ajar.

A JELLICLE CAT

December is the cruellest month –
The goat coughs in the field above:
The nights are far too bleak for hunting,
For strolling, or for making love.

Arcturus and the frozen Bear
Prowl in the circumpolar sky:
I call upon my friend, the poet,
In hopes, at least, of cold game-pie.

Through a convenient open window
I slip, insidious as sin –
St Louis – Harvard – Kensington
The accents which he greets me in.

Curled up beside the electric fire,
I take my ease in his abode:
The alley strays are caterwauling
Around St Stephen's, Gloucester Road,

As once they joined their desolate cries
Round bright Apollo's Theban fane,
To those of blinded Oedipus,
When truth, at last, was all too plain.

TIME PIECES

to John Cherrington

ALARM CLOCK

Woolworths or Marks and Sparks my stable –
My face is friendly but uncompromising,
A bold, unambiguous circle of Arabic numerals,
My voice a little hammer on a tinny anvil.
Destroyer of dreams, and enemy
Of self-indulgent slumber,
I summon you into the real world –
You have a date with Philip Larkin's toad.

GRANDFATHER CLOCK

I mark not hours and quarters only,
But generations, reigns – Edward, Victoria, George.
Before I strike, I clear my throat,
And grind, and groan, and belch:
My voice is patriarchal, magisterial.
My countenance seems kindly, assimilated
In some strange manner to the family face,
Which always changes and is still the same.
My glass and my brass fittings gleam,
Cherished by footmen and by housemaids.
If they neglected it, the Lares –
English Hobs and Lobs – had done the chore
Between the noon of night and cock-crow.

VICTORIAN WATCH AND CHAIN

I was great uncle Roger Podger's watch,
Attentive to duty, reliable, and solid.
Mincing Lane and Leadenhall Street knew me.
My bright silver chain was slung
Across his belly, comfortably replete
With bacon and eggs, and porridge,
Roast beef, mutton chops, and Stilton cheese,
Buttered muffins, semolina pudding;
But I lay snug inside his waistcoat pocket,
Close bosom crony to his heart,
Whose tick concurred with mine:
"Time is money, money is truth and truth
Is prosperous respectability."

A LADY'S WRISTWATCH

My voice is so small, you scarcely notice it,
Extending your hand in the minuet –
Or is it the disco jive?
Yet it ticks faster than the running seconds,
Telling how youth departs, and love, and beauty.
I am a silver leech, that's fastened
Over your bluest vein –
The one that tracks directly to your heart.

CUCKOO CLOCK

I'm Swiss culture's finest flower:
Kleines vöglein tells the hour;
As his door wide open swings,
Hark, le petit oiseau sings;
Mark il piccolo uccello's
Voice, that's worked by tiny bellows
(Since the little birdie's Swiss,
He's tri-lingual too, like this).

Winter, springtime, summer, fall,
You can hear the cuckoo call,
Which is, Shakespeare makes quite clear,
Bad news for a married ear,
Hinting at a faithless wife.
But the man of single life
Knows, still more than he who's married,
Time for no man ever tarried.

CLASSROOM CLOCK

It hangs on the wall, a round unsmiling O
(Euclid of Megara might have seen beauty there).
Its hands move on, inexorable
As the slow tread of Caesar's legionaries
Reciting the principal parts of Latin verbs:
"Venio venire veni ventum,
Video videre vidi visum,
Vinco vincere vici victum."
The minutes stretch ahead like multiplication tables,
Or like recurring decimals,
Like dates of English kings, or lists
Of those of Israel and of Judah,
Who mostly did evil in the sight of the Lord
And came to nasty ends.

A clangorous bell shall signal your release:
Meantime the playing fields are green,
Or trampled to mud.
Innumerable and innumerate leaves
Are fluttering on the tree-boughs;
The birds that sing there never heard of syntax.

DANDELION CLOCK

Here in the dandelion fields of childhood
Time is contained in a few puffs of breath;
Here no devourer blunts the lion's tooth.
Your marriage date, and all your life's vocation,
Is measured out in cherry stones,
And lovers' luck's foretold
By the torn, scattered petals of a daisy.

INSCRIPTION FOR A SUNDIAL

I note the bright hours' passing. Those that are dark,
And overclouded ones, I cannot mark:
That they are likewise winged, and must depart,
Is measured only by the trusting heart.

EGG-TIMER

A cute little man in a cute little chef's high hat,
Is grasping a cute little hour glass, the attribute
Of child-devouring Chronos (Goya painted him
To brighten up his dining room), or else
Formerly it measured out the parson's sermon,
On Death and Judgment maybe, Hell and possibly Heaven –
But this is for the boiling of an egg,
A little world congealing like our world,
Only a bit quicker.

Four and a half minutes is the optimum,
But not at four and a half thousand feet above sea level –
In Mexico City for instance, where I witnessed
A comedy played out in the restaurant
Of my hotel – an American lady
Rejecting, time after time, the egg which had been boiled,
At her request, four and a half minutes flat,
But at that altitude was nearly liquid.

There are some circles, I am told,
In which they never use an egg-timer:
They just put on a record
Of Mozart's 'Marriage of Figaro' Overture,
Which lasts, as every good conductor knows,
Just the required time.

TIM

Alas for TIM! My muse weep now for TIM –
Timandra was she then or Timothea,
Or else Diotima. Though some maintain
TIM was no more than a recorded voice,
We others knew the truth and pitied her:
That hapless girl, imprisoned for long years
Within the most obscure and dismal dungeon,
Deep down beneath the General Post Office,
Compelled to speak the time each thirtieth second.
They lured her there with specious promises,
Those hard-faced bureaucrats, and praised her taste
When she recited to the Poet Laureate,
Mr John Masefield, some well-chosen lines
Taken from Milton's works – his blithe *L'Allegro*.
But she no more would greet the cheerful day,
Or listen to the soaring lark at dawn,
Singing from his watchtower in the skies.
And when at last Death brought to her release,
They buried her in clammy London clay
At dead of midnight. Psalm, nor dirge, nor prayer
Whispered above her grave, though some report
A stealthy tear was quivering in the eye
Of that stern tyrant, the Postmaster General.

And now instead we have a horrid robot
Whose name apparently is Accurist.
I need no time that Accurist can sponsor –
It's God alone who sponsors time for me.

PUB CLOCK

Hurry along now, it's time!
The pinball machine
Ceases to flash and the juke-box to blare;
Even the Space Invaders have
Temporarily called off their project.
The tropical fish excitedly
Swim to and fro inside their lighted fish tank.
As in the days of Noah, they recognise the signals
That they will soon be fed.

I know I'm a liar, I know
That I am always exactly ten minutes fast –
It's the only feasible way to get rid of you lot.
Go gulp and gargle down your Guinnesses,
Your bitters, your browns, your lagers and limes;
Sling down your gins, sup up your scotches,
And out with you into the ambient darkness,
Into unfriendly streets. And please remember
To me it's a matter of total indifference
Whether you stagger home to a snug bed,
Or end up under a bus, or topple
Into a ditch and drown.

See you all tomorrow night!

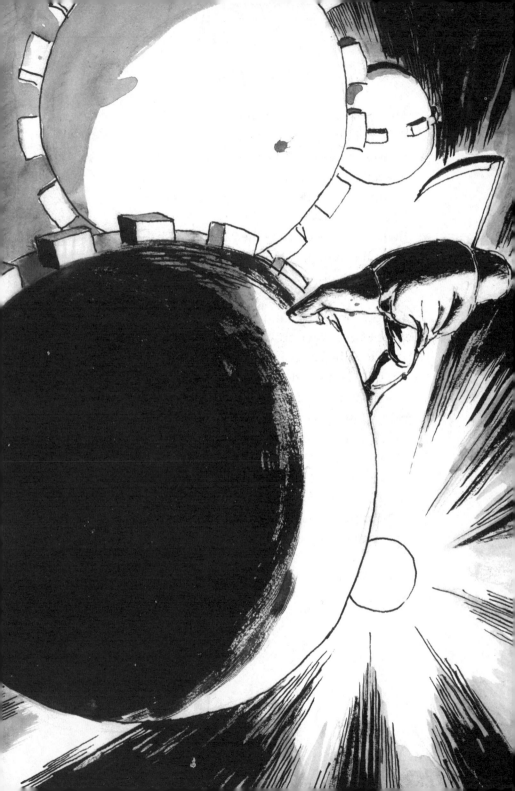

THE COSMIC CLOCK

Planets, stars, galaxies – the whole
Winking and blinking caboodle –
This, it seems, is the only reliable clock:
A beam from a star crossed a sensitive plate –
Then came the pips: the British nation
Turned on the ten o'clock news.

This is the moving image of eternity –
I don't mean Paley's watch, discarded
By the absconding Watchmaker
Upon a bank of Wordsworthian daffodils,
But pulsars, quasars, decaying elements, black holes;
Yet this, they say, is likewise winding down –
And hickory-dickory, men and mice we run in it!

A PARTRIDGE IN A PEAR TREE

On the first day of Christmas my true love sent to me ...

A PARTRIDGE IN A PEAR TREE

A partridge perched on a pear-tree bough
On Christmas day – *une jolie perdriz*:
She had grown plump on stubble-gleaning
In September, and had dodged the guns.

Bare the branches now, but when spring comes
Leaves shall deck them and at summer's close
Depending pears, great tears of musky sweetness.

On the second day of Christmas my true love sent to me ...

TWO TURTLE DOVES

I send the image of two turtle-doves,
A token of fidelity. They do not flutter here
In cold December, under English skies.
In due time they'll be back with other migrants
From climes more southerly. First will come the chiffchaff;
Then in May
The laggard fern-owl and the tardy turtle:
Tur-tur, tur-tur, tur-tur, be heard
About the land, a soft murmuring,
Amid profusion of the spring-time flowers.

On the third day of Christmas my true love sent to me ...

THREE FRENCH HENS

Honorine, Alphonsine, and Pertelot –
Three French hens, scrabble and scrape
For groundsel and ground-ivy in the gravel.
They cluck and chuckle disapprovingly
About *ce méchant Monsieur Chanticler*
And all his goings-on; the *affreuse* malice
Of that hunchbacked guinea-fowl,
Her widow's black sewn with pearls for tears;
And that canard canaille,
The waddling and mud-dabbling ducks and ducklings.

On the fourth day of Christmas my true love sent to me ...

FOUR CALLING BIRDS

Four birds calling and crying
In December twilight –
Four colly birds, four coal-black blackbirds –
'Tack, tack, tack, tack, tack!'
Through the leafless wood, till roosting time.

On the fifth day of Christmas my true love sent to me ...

FIVE GOLD RINGS

Five golden circles wed
Your senses to the outer world. One is for sight –
Sun-rays, marigold, fields of oil-seed rape,
The yellowhammer's feathers, eyes
Of lace-wing and of gadfly. One is for sound –
Gold blare of the trumpet, harp strings,
Gold-billed blackbird's song, and voices
Of those you loved, in dreams. And one for scent –
Perfume of mignonette,
And of the gorse that blooms on the summer heath,
And brandy-bottle yellow water-lily.
One for all rich and exquisite flavours –
Buttered haddock, Gloucester cheese, omelettes,
Pamplemousse, honey, saffron cake. And one
For the cold hard feel you get from gold itself.

On the sixth day of Christmas my true love sent to me ...

SIX GEESE A-LAYING

Six geese stepping upon the green,
Honking and hissing – they will scare away
All the tedious and quotidian devils
That fret at your life, or cling to it like goose-grass
(Juno's geese it was that saved the Capitol)
And, if you're very lucky,
Before the year is over,
There's one that's going to lay the alchemical egg.

On the seventh day of Christmas my true love sent to me ...

SEVEN SWANS A-SWIMMING

Seven wild swans are floating
Under a bleak sky, over a waste sea.
Another year comes round, and still
No end to their continual exile here.

These are Lir's children, changed
To wild whooping swans, that whistling call
Their desolate lament. Only a Christian bell, a hermit's bell
Chiming for matins or for evensong
Over the noisy waves, shall break
That black enchantment and restore them
To human form, human companionship.

On the eighth day of Christmas my true love sent to me ...

EIGHT MAIDS A-MILKING

"Where are you going, this frosty morning,
My eight mawthers?" "To the cattle-byre.
Our cows need milking – Dapple and Whitesocks,
Buttercup, Moondaisy, Tulip and Sorrel,
Periwinkle and Crumplehorn. The milk and the cream
Are wanted for junkets and syllabubs,
Cheesecakes and flummery, for the Twelfth Night feast –
It's not far off now."

On the ninth day of Christmas my true love sent to me ...

NINE LADIES DANCING

They dance by the frozen lake, a silver mirror
For the great winter moon and for the stars.
Their dance is light and darkness, day and night-time,
Winter and spring, the summer and the autumn,
Man's birth, man's life, man's death – they are nine witches,
Nine white witches in a shining midnight.

On the tenth day of Christmas my true love sent to me ...

TEN LORDS A-LEAPING

Ten lords come rushing in, tripping and skipping;
Kicking up their heels they whoop and halloo.
Each takes a lady by the hand – there are nine ladies:
Lord Prance, Lord Hopfrog, and Lord Salar Salmon,
Lord Jiminy Cricket, and Lord Merrygrig,
All choose their partners – so do brisk Lord Wallaby,
Lord Capriole, Lord Pulex, and Lord Highjump.
One, two, three, hop! – see them dance the polka,
Lavolta, piedz-en-l'air and saltarello,
Trepaks and gopaks – all the jumping dances!
There's only one lord cannot find a lady –
Lord Oddmanout – and he must leap alone.

On the eleventh day of Christmas my true love sent to me ...

ELEVEN PIPERS PIPING

Eleven shepherds piped around a manger.
Eleven days have passed, and they must take their leave.
Their bagpipe tunes are fading, as they go
Back to the high hills, where linger still
Reverberations of the angels' song.

On the twelfth day of Christmas my true love sent to me ...

TWELVE DRUMMERS DRUMMING

Twelve drummers, twelve African drummers:
Ostrich plumes nod over their locks;
Lion skins and monkey tails drape
Their naked shoulders; barbaric blazing rubies
Gleam on the shining blackness of their chests.

Three kings march towards Bethlehem,
With gifts of gold and spices, and the third
Is Balthasar of Ethiopia
With his medicine-herb. These are his entourage;
Their talking rhythms make articulate
Surge of the blood, the rising of the sap,
A sacrificial dance of death in spring,
Thunder of resurrection, and beyond it
The rushing of a pentecostal wind.

A NINEFOLD OF CHARMS

for Adam Johnson

TO GET RID OF A MOUSE

Out of the house, mouse – esurient rodent,
Squeaking, scrabbling, scuttling, micturating
Don Whiskerandos – scram, skidaddle, vamoose, imshi!

By all the wholesome dishes you've polluted,
By all the innocent slumbers
Your scratchings discomposed,
By all the hapless virgins you've besieged,
Who leapt on chairs and tables, skirts drawn up,
By all the manuscripts of verses –
Sole bid for fame of starve-in-a-garret poets –
You shredded to make more snug
Your all too procreant and prolific nest:

Against you I invoke
Apollo Smintheus in Olympian terrors,
The shadow of a giant farmer's wife
Carver in hand, whetted for amputation,
The Hamelin piper, and I summon
Grimalkin ghosts and phantom ferrets,
And grieving spirits of those Irish rats
That once were rhymed to death. In vain
You call for aid upon your ancestors
Fallen in Homeric struggle against
The clammy legions of the frogs –

Batrachomyomachia, there's
A word to conjure with, and if
All this doesn't work it must be traps,
Next time it must be poison.

AGAINST A RAT

Rattus norvegicus, your name disgraces
The homeland of Ibsen and of Grieg,
But you came sneaking out of Tartary
In the stinking holds of Muscovy ships,
And now you inhabit dishonoured London –
Dishonoured by piles of foetid garbage,
Bones of chickens that never saw Kentucky,
Only the inside of a battery-prison,
Greasy chip-papers, half-eaten hamburgers,
All the detritus of fast, so-called food.
Creep back to the sewers you've come from –
If your troglodyte brothers there will accept you.
I'll bandy no more verses with you, you git –
So just git!

TO INHIBIT THE BREEDING OF MAGGOTS IN A CHEESE

Some people, I know, regard you as a delicacy.
There was, I recall, a heretical sect
That held the world one great ripe cheese
And men the maggots in it. But, for my part,
I'd have my double Gloucester, my Caerphilly,
Sage Derby, Wensleydale or Cheddar,
A wedge-shaped slice of a sterile world,
Lifeless as the glassy, green-cheese moon.

TO DISCOURAGE A SPIDER FROM GETTING
INTO THE BATH

Inzy-winzy, dingy widow –
Though you ate your husband, you're a careful mother.
Therefore I think kindly of you, though
There are others who don't.

Those smooth enamelled precipices,
The sides of the soapy, scummy bath-tub,
More treacherous than the Leucadian cliff
That Sappho leapt from – once down there
There'll be, spider, no climbing out,
And, ineluctably, a sudden scalding deluge
May sweep you down, like a dark eight-rayed star,
Finally vanishing into its black hole.

FOR THE APPLE ORCHARD

Apple trees, old apple trees,
Take a wassail, if you please
To accept it, as we bring
Cider for your christening;
Bits of toast we'll leave there then,
For the robin and the wren,
And, before we go, discharge
Rounds of shot, to scare at large
Spirits of infecundity,
Skulking, loitering by each tree.
Aphis, codlin moth, and scale,
Hence! And hence, cold corn of hail.
Moderate be the wind and rain,
As the months come round again;
Sunshine bless you still, and let
Bees industriously set
Blossom, till the bounteous year
Bring its gift of apples here –
Red and sweet, or sharp and green,
For apple-bobbing Halloween;
Pippins, Bramleys – every kind
Memory can call to mind.

We shall get them, by and by,
In apple-pudding, apple pie,
Apple dumplings, and the humble
Turnover, and apple-crumble,
Apple stewed with cinnamon,
Or baked and stuffed, – shall I go on?
That for such our mother Eve
Lost Eden, we may well believe.

Praise all apples then, and bless
That which spurts out of the press,
And matures in cask or tun,
Exiled from the fervid sun:
Cider – rather say divine
Pomona's gold and amber wine!

Thralled by that Hesperian boon,
Often, underneath the moon,
Treading on enchanted ground,
We have gone the long way round,
Tangle-footed, pixie-led,
Totty-pated, home to bed.

A LOVE CHARM

Hard as a quince, dreamy and decadent as a medlar,
Crisp as an apple, sweet and gritty like a pear –
A pear that is going sleepy,
Smooth and slippery as an eel, quick as a silverfish,
Prickly as a horse-chestnut in its case,
Or as a burr, or clinging goose-grass,
Singing and soaring, like a skylark,
Towards the cumuli, plummeting
Like a hawk to her prey, brash as a sparrow
Dust-bathing in the midst of the high road,
Erratic as a dancing butterfly, committed
As a wood-ant foraging among the pine-needles,
Prompt as a taxi on call, or as the post,
Dodgy and unpredictable as a roulette wheel,
Dilatory as a summer afternoon
For punting or canoeing up the river,
Brisk as a September wind
With a touch of frost in it, drifting like thistledown,
Or like the soft fluff of rose-bay
Growing from earth that fire has ravaged,
Distant as a bright star, nearer than the jugular,
Haunting as a half-remembered dream,
Or a ghostly whiff of perfume, or the snatch of a tune –
All these I would have you be, and when these images
At last have been counted, have been discarded,
Fallible, wounded, human.

FOR UNBLOCKING THE SINK

I have plunged with the plunger, I have poked
With a piece of bent wire, and still
This obstinate outlet is blocked –
Blocked with scraps of potato peelings,
With the outer leaves of sprouts, congealed fat,
Spent matches, and shreds
Of plastic packagings no doubt,
With roughage of coffee grounds and tea leaves,
Like discarded parts of my own life
I would rather forget, clogging my consciousness.

Therefore, Cloacina, you I invoke –
Venerable goddess whom Rome honoured,
Whom London, with every city, must –
Regent of sewers and drains, somewhere
Among the underground rivers, deep
In the obscure of a winding labyrinth, must be
Your throne of ordures, where you sit,
Nimbused by methane, and about you scattered
Heaps of lost treasures, and rejected things.
Without your workings no civility stands:
Man stifles in his own effluent,
The rat, the cockroach, and the carrion crow
Finally triumph, and an invisible angel
Beats dark and fiery wings
About our streets and towers and terraces.
Your aid I implore then – up through this choked pipe
Send gargle and gurgle and gulp,
And bubbles rising, with the joyful sound
Of waters running free. If not,
I'll send down the contents of a can
Of caustic soda – it is not a gift
I care to present to a lady.

FOR A COUGH

Frog in my throat, frog in my throat,
Jump out, hopalong, ploppity plop;
Return, you clammy phlegm-green gentleman
To your Lethean lake.

Homely onion soup will mollify,
Likewise the small blue squill,
Horehound and tussilago
With its yellow flowers and great flat leaves
Broad as a colt's foot but downy beneath.

Garlic also is sovereign,
Though it will never turn me into Caruso.
But being rid of you, frog, I at least
Can mouth my verses from the podium.

TO INDUCE SLEEP

Each hair of my head severally I relax
My nose I relax, my teeth, and my navel,
And my ten toes like ten little piglets;
Envisage an endless procession
Of silly, woolly, bleating innocents
Whose only purpose in life is just to be counted.
I call on the poppy-crowned Morpheus,
With his leaden mace and his clavichord
Playing continually the Goldberg variations,
To snatch me past the safety-curtain of dreams
Down to the darkness, down to the deep,
Deep sleep, sleep deep, deep, deep, deep sleep.

THE PARSON'S CAT

PROLOGUE

"The parson's cat is an angry cat.
The parson's cat is a busy cat.
The parson's cat is a curious cat.
The parson's cat's a delightful cat ..."
Reader, did you ever play
This Victorian game? I'll not bore you
By going through all the six-and-twenty letters
Which make our alphabet. I'll just choose eight,
And they'll spell out his hidden name
(A name of horror and terror it is to boot –
The parson's cat is the shadow of the parson).

So, with this little saucer of hors d'oeuvre,
In all there'll be nine poems, or whatever they are –
One for each of his nine lives.

THE PARSON'S CAT IS A BEAUTIFUL CAT

"A beautiful cat, a blessed cat," so says his master,
The Reverend Simon Simplex – if cats have masters
(It's a moot point).
A brash, bumptious Bob's-your-uncle cat.

When God created Cat He created
Elegance and stealth, beauty and ruthlessness,
The silent skill to stalk, to pounce
To finish off.

When He created Dog, He created
Pack-fidelity, and the tenaciousness
To run down prey to exhaustion,
To tear apart.

"Dog is my friend" said Adam.
After the Expulsion when all beasts shunned him,
And he sat moping, something licked his hand.
It was the dog.

So while Adam continued to sit there,
Still moping, sentimentally fondling his dog,
Eve began to tame their new environment,
Devising the sowing, the reaping, the threshing of corn,
The garnering into barns. And where you store corn
You get mice. And where you get mice the cat will come.

"Cat is my friend," said Eve "to be partaker
Of my nocturnal, secret, moonlight mysteries."

THE PARSON'S CAT IS AN AMOROUS CAT

A handsome fellow and a lady-killer,
As Pushkinova, Zuleika and Shireen,
Princess Miu of Siam and Tibaldina,
With all the other side-street malkin minxes
Can testify. But they
Were anyone's little bits of fluff.

His real passion was for Lady Pouncewell.
She lived up the hill at Horner's Hall,
A decayed Jacobean mansion. William Wycherley
Had slept there once, so had the Earl of Rochester,
And as it happens alone. So she affected
A Restoration pose, would twitch her tail
With an air, like Millamant's fan.

The parson's cat would nightly serenade her:
 Pretty-puss-Pouncewell I must worship
 Your whiskery face, each steel-sharp claw;
 Pity your poor lover, shivering
 Out in the winter wind so raw!

She, in good voice, joined the duet:
 Mi-ow-oo! Pssst!
Although she vowed she'd rather far be singing
An air of Henry Purcell, or John Eccles,
Or the great Doctor Blow.

THE PARSON'S CAT IS A PREACHING CAT

The clock in the tower chimes midnight.
Dressed in hood and surplice, the Parson's cat
Climbs up the pulpit steps.
He preaches to a congregation
Of church mice. He bids them always mind
Their P's and Q's, to be content
With what small crumbs may fall upon the floor for them;
And never to raid the larder or the sideboard,
Never to steal food. And if they're good
Of course they'll go to Heaven, when they are safely dead.
And Heaven is a great unlimited cheese-pie

   High up in the sky.
"Please," squeaked one small dissident mouse
"We would much rather it was a chocolate pudding."
The parson's cat withered him with a look,
Then gave the blessing. And as they all filed out
Could not resist pouncing upon the last mouse –
It was the tenth. He snapped her spine,
And – crunch! – he swallowed her,
That was his supper, or was it an early breakfast?

THE PARSON'S CAT IS A HOMELY CAT

The kettle is on the hob. Muffins are toasting.
Outside, it's a late twilight, gusty with rain.
But indoors, warmth, security, English comfort.
The clock ticks on, as if that time
Would never have a stop. In another room
Someone is practising a piece by Mendelssohn.

The cat lies by the fire and seems asleep.
But one eye is open. Listen, do you not hear
That steady, gentle purring?
Claws under the velvet.

THE PARSON'S CAT IS AN OCCULTIST CAT

The parson makes ready the church
For tomorrow's service. It will be All Saints.
Through gates of pearl the countless host shall stream.
But the parson's cat is nowhere to be found.
All Hallowe'en! He's sneaked off
Unobserved, to Bald Top Mountain.
Mrs Circe Henbane and her coven
Perform Satanic rites. Two other cats
Have met him there. One is called Pertinax.
The other is Smokey Jim. They are assistants,
And tend the little fires that burn
Lucidly blue and green or dirty yellow,
Fed with nitrous impurities and certain herbs
Gathered at midnight – slips of churchyard yew,
Mugwort, yarrow and enchanter's nightshade.
Then the fiddle strikes up and the dance begins.
Warlocks and witches and cats and all
Twirl in a widdershins lavolta. And they send up,
To the red hunter's moon,
A wild, promiscuous, loveless yowling.

THE PARSON'S CAT IS A MOON CAT

In the early days of space exploration,
Before Gagarin or Major Glenn,
They sent up modules and nodules,
Capsules and sputniks and other contraptions,
Crewed by beings with less than human consciousness:
A sprouting bed of asparagus, orb-weaving spiders,
Or a little Russian dog called Bitter Lemon.
The parson's cat had heard rumours of this,
He was of an exploring turn of mind.
Having passed security guards, he found
One of these cosmic gadgets just lying about.
In he slipped, unmarked.
The thing was blasted off,
And duly landed on the polished face
Of the round shining moon. The cat
Quietly disembarked. No one had noticed,
Except possibly the moon herself
Who turned, for an unobtrusive moment,
A pale shade of blue.

A small black dot, too tiny
For any telescope to pick out,
The parson's cat
Strolled (one big step for felinity)
About those frigid, glassy mountains,
Those undynamic craters, waterless seas.

"I never subscribed" he said
"To the made-of-green-cheese hypothesis,
But I had dreamed of moon-mice –
Little translucent creatures with spindly jerboa-like legs
And six wings resembling those of mayfly,
To flutter and skip about these barren hills,
And moon-birds likewise,
Pearly white similar to nightjars
With eight great staring eyes, and long extensile tongues
Such as humming-birds are furnished with.
I glimpse no flitting, I catch no bleep of either –
No happy hunting-ground this lunar landscape."

And how did he get back? The question's easy –
Mrs Circe Henbane just happened to be passing.
She gave him a lift on her broomstick.

THE PARSON'S CAT IS AN EPICUREAN CAT

The parson's cat is fond of fish,
Served in a little porcelain dish,
Although of coley, cod, or hake,
He will not willingly partake;
But salmon steaks, he says, and trout
He finds it hard to do without –
Oysters too, and anchovies.
He fancies certain kinds of cheese –
Camembert or Port Salut –
But ordinary cheddar you
Might bait a mouse-trap with, won't do.
Chicken he likes, but just the best –
Only the white meat of the breast.
Fresh milk he holds in high esteem –
If it's enriched with double cream;
And puddings, as a general rule –
Crème brûlée or gooseberry fool.

You'll say "If a poor parson's cat
Gets food like this, I'll eat my hat!"
The parson, not to be ambiguous
Enjoys a stipend quite exiguous;
And he dispenses at his door
Half that to the local poor.
Fasting and abstinence in Lent
Strictly observes – such is his bent;
And then his board may only boast
Plain lentil soup, or beans on toast,
But God forbid that he, a priest,
Force fasting on the unfallen beast.
Yet, feast or fast, throughout the year,
He dishes out quite simple fare,
Suitable for a parson's cat –
Fish-heads, and lites, and things like that.

Dishes of another kind
The cat may taste, but in his mind,
While he is dozing by the fire,
Haunted by images of desire.
In a soft, sweet, sensual dream
His pink tongue laps up double cream,
Tastes chicken breasts, and – I've no doubt –
Salmon steaks and rainbow trout.

Besides there is an end in view –
A moggie has a job to do,
Must have an appetite not too nice –
He's got to rid the place of mice.

THE PARSON'S CAT IS A TERRITORIAL CAT

"I'm sick of the country" said red Reynard
"Poison, pollution, traps, guns –
That's all it is. And most the infamous hunt –
Riffraff in spurious pink,
And at their heels
The sycophantic baying of the pack.
They dig out one, they stop up earths,
Throw one to the tearing of the fangs.
Themselves are blood-baptised, they call it sport.

"It was different perhaps in England's dreamtime,
When they hunted the sun at midsummer
Out of the harvest field, and horn-calls music
Would blow away the morning dew. But now – Ough!

"I will go to the town," he said, "I will change my name.
I shall be Urban Fox. There in the dustbins,
I'm told, there are rich pickings.
For there is nothing the affluent and upwardly-mobile
Enjoy more than throwing away good food –
While they let drop a mildly crocodilian tear
For the Ethiopian starving."

So he trotted along the tarmac at dawn,
Sneaked by hedgerows, where there were still hedgerows,
Along dry ditches, until at length he came
To what had been a village, now engulfed
By spreading suburban sprawl.

He entered, so it chanced, the vicarage garden,
But there he encountered a horror,
A monster – the parson's cat
With hair on end fluffed up
To double his size, tail erect like a bottle-brush,
Claws unretracted, spitting hatred and anger
And, as it seemed, poison.

"Out!" said the cat. "You dog. This is my patch.
Out, you filthy sandy-haired stinking tyke!"
"I beg your pardon," said the fox, "I am no dog.
See, I have eyes that wax and wane
Like yours in the light and darkness.
We two ought to be allies.
As for my stink, you can ask the hounds about that.
It is totally alien from them. They itch
To tear me limb from limb."

"Dog you are," said the cat "and as dog you'll go!
And that applies to Brock, your crony, too!"
"Why, clearly he's no canine." "Half weasel and half bear
That he may be! But still I'll see him off,
As I would the great, frozen, starry Bear himself
Prowling around Polaris
Through the long darkness of the winter nights.
So off with you dog-fox or else you'll feel
My talons in your waxing, waning eyes,
The points of my teeth in the base of your brittle spine."
The fox, Sir Urban Fox, strategically
Withdrew. He knew when he wasn't welcome.

CHIMAERAS

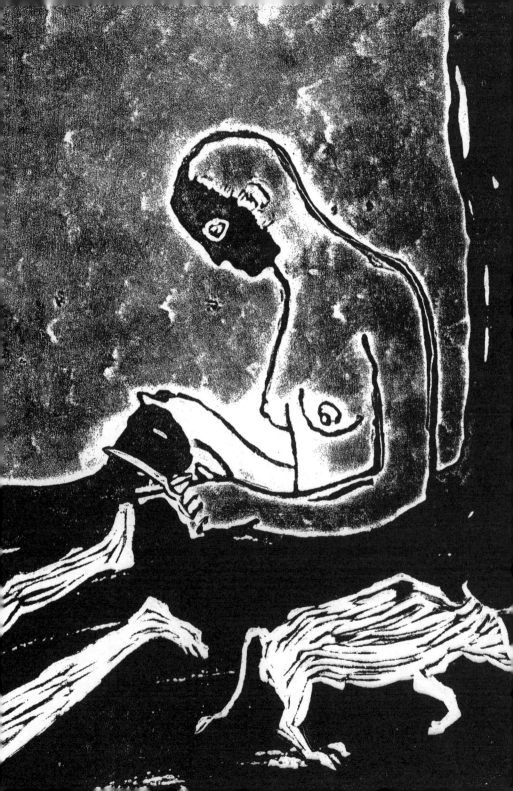

CHIMAERAS – THEIR ORIGINS

Celestial Sophia sat enthroned
Within the darkness of the Unknown God.
It was the Sixth Day, and she was busy
Sewing and snipping, and cutting out patterns –
Patterns of quadrupeds, beasts and cattle,
Serpents, alligators, human beings.
The selfish genes, her servants,
And the environmental factors
Stood by to work those patterns out.
But there were remnants which they rejected –
Heads and tails, wings and limbs and claws.
They drifted into the trashcan of the Cosmos.

Beelzebub, Lucifer and their confederates
The Rebel Angels had all been swept there
Some days previously. The babyish devils
Delighted in those anonymous fragments,
Creating chimaeras, beasts discordantly made up
Of incompatible parts – as hippogriffs,
Sphinxes, bucentaurs, tragopans,
Gorgons and cockatrices.
But the devils soon matured
And got engrossed in a more adult project –
The engineering of the Fall of Man.

Discarded now, the chimaeras
Still bombinated in their vacuum.

LYCIAN CHIMAERA: BELLEROPHON ON PEGASUS

One beast climbed out of the vacuum,
Scouted around the mountains of Asia Minor,
Incinerating cornfields, vineyards, apple-orchards,
Barbecuing livestock, not to speak
Of little shepherd boys. Its three heads breathed
Miasmas of the seasons – out of the lion's came
The parching heat of summer, from the serpent's
The sicknesses of autumn, from the goat's
The biting winter frosts. It was Bellerophon
Settled its bacon. The thrice three Muses
Descended from Mount Helicon, fingering
Their archlutes, hautboys, hurdy-gurdies.
"We've brought you a present," they said,
"Our wonderful winged horse,
Our darling Pegasus, born from the Gorgon's blood.
Mount to his saddle, and quash
The obscene tricephalous blob." And so he did.

STHENO AND EURYALE

Medusa had two sisters,
And they were madly jealous of her.
Her terrible beauty could turn men to stone,
And they could do that likewise, but, foul as pigs,
No one would look at them.

When Perseus snipped Medusa's head off
The other two were on his track –
But he outpaced them with his fluttering sandals –
They'd sworn to tear him limb from bloody limb.

Even among monsters
Family values count.

THE THEBAN SPHINX

Her last riddle, the one
Oedipus did not solve was this:
That she herself, winged lion with a pitiless face,
Was also royal Jocasta, who would finish
Hanging from a palace beam, a hempen neckinger
Around her delicate throat.

But it was enough, he had demonstrated
That he was a king, a cunning man,
Clever enough to be the bridegroom
Of Turandot, or Antiochus's daughter.

THE CENTAUR CHEIRON

Cheiron, the good centaur,
Founded a prototype Public School,
High in a cave on the mountains,
An academy for heroes.

His graduates included
Much-labouring, much-enduring Hercules;
Peleus who subdued
Shape-shifting Thetis, a mermaid,
Half cephalopod, half goddess
(And from their union sprang
Achilles of the resonant war-whoop);
Jason too, who opened up,
Over the dark waves of the Euxine,
The sea-road to the land of golden fleeces:
He exploited the gold and exploited women – Dante
Put him in hell for a seducer.

Heroes sack cities, found empires, occasionally
Leave codes of useful laws.

They need all the human wisdom they can get,
And a deal of horse sense too.

THE ANT-LION

A lion prowling on the wide savannahs
Met up with an ant – an exiled queen
Who'd strayed far from her formicarian city.
He fell in love, and she returned his passion.
In spite of obvious incompatabilities
Of taste and size, their love was consummated.
Their offspring was the ant-lion – a strange chimaera,
Who had his father's head and mane and terrible fangs,
Shoulders and taloned fore-paws too – but, turn him round
There was the ant's slim waist, and bulbous abdomen –
Two pairs of spindly hindlegs in addition.

The lion had fed on bleeding hunks of flesh,
Torn from the zebra and the wildebeest
Ranging those plains. The little ant preferred
Small scraps of sweetness she could forage for,
Among the fallen debris of the woodlands:
Exiguous seeds and tiny mushrooms, likewise
Soft plump maggots. She sipped honey-dew
Workers had milked for her from herds of green-fly
Sucking the juices of the summer rose.

And thus it came about the ant-lion,
Which might have been a creature you could dream of –
A counsellor and friend of man, combining
The noble lion's courage with the pismire's
Prudence and industry – simply because
What his forequarters slew and swallowed down
His hinder parts could not digest, was doomed to die
Of malnutrition or a stomach-ache.

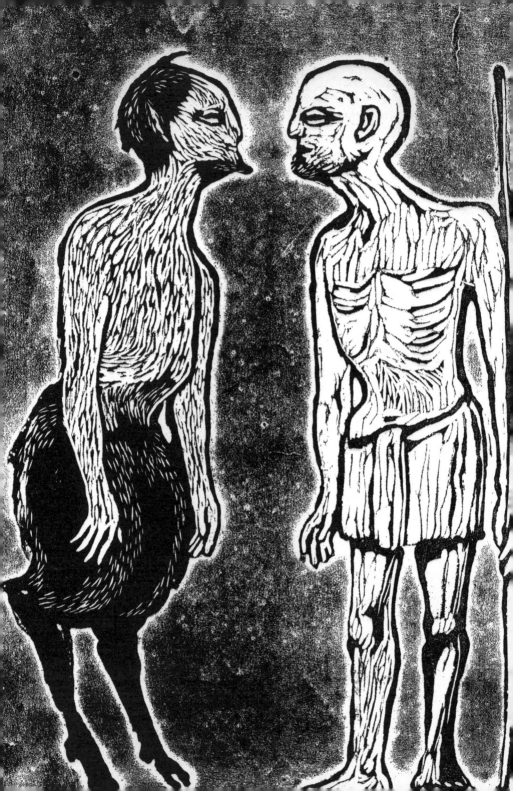

SAINT ANTHONY OF EGYPT AND THE SATYR

"If you're looking for the cell of your friend,
Saint Paul the Hermit," said the Satyr
"Turn left at the next clump of palm trees,
And then turn right at the derelict tomb
Of King Seti the Second, then keep on
With the Dog Star right in front of you,
And after about ten hours you'll come
To a small reed hut. That is his hermit-hold.
And whisper a prayer for me too, won't you,
As you go trudging on." "I know your kind,"
Replied Saint Anthony, "There's one preserved in salt
In the Museum in Alexandria.
You are Cain's kin, who somehow or other
Survived the Flood. Or else
The offspring of abominable lusts –
Men shagging nanny-goats or upland mares,
Begetting satyrs thus and centaurs.
There's no prayers for the likes of you, although
I'm grateful for your courteous directions."

And so the saint stalked on, but as he went
Muttered a tiny prayer for the hirsute satyr,
Or cynocephalus baboon or whatever it was –
Though feeling not quite sure he really ought to.

But when he reached his friend Saint Paul the Hermit,
Who was older than he was and holier too,
He mentioned the encounter, while they shared
Four dried dates between them for their supper.
"Of course you were right to pray," replied Saint Paul
"There's no such thing as a wasted prayer, brother."

UNICORN

With silver hooves and silken mane
  And spiral-twisted ivory horn,
Upon the crystal mountains trots
  The solitary unicorn.

Nor gin nor snare can trip his heels,
  Nor is he any huntsman's game:
Immaculately chaste, a virgin
  Alone can make that creature tame.

Beneath a sumptuous canopy
  A king of kings sat down to dine:
His most belov'd and trusted friend
  Stood by to fill his cup with wine.

His trusted friend? He should have known
  There's none that gold cannot suborn:
A deadly and slow-working poison
  Was slipped into his cup of horn.

Of unicorn horn that cup was fashioned,
  With cabbalistic signs engraved.
It splintered to a thousand pieces –
  But a royal life was saved.

And soon the traitors stood revealed
  Who'd plotted to snuff out that life –
The trusted friend who bore his cup,
  His son, his vizier, and his wife.

But on the far off crystal mountains,
  With blood-stained and dishonoured brow,
Snared by a young girl's chastity,
  The unicorn is weeping now.

THE KING OF THE HERRINGS

There's one chimaera that doesn't belong here –
Part of the natural world, not that of myth –
An oddball fish, a Palaeozoic survivor,
A sort of poor relation of the sharks,
Perhaps of the coelocanth. *Chimaera monstrosa*
Linnaeus named him. He goes before the herring shoals –
With his rabbitty mouth and disappointing tail –
Known to trawlermen as 'King of the Herrings'.
No use to take him in their nets –
He'll never be a kipper or a bloater.

Soft and hard roes alike, the herrings treat him
With honour and respect, I'm sure:
But I wouldn't like to repeat
What some of those brash young sprats and pilchards
Say about him behind his back.

These poems are taken from the original pamphlets by John Heath-Stubbs, with all
the original illustrations by Emily Johns, and are available from booksellers. In case
of difficulty in obtaining these, or for a complete list of Hearing Eye publications,
please write enclosing an s.a.e. to:
Hearing Eye, Box 1, 99 Torriano Avenue, London NW5 2RX